HOMOSEXUALITY
"IT'S NOT WHAT YOU
THINK IT IS"

HOMOSEXUALITY "IT'S NOT WHAT YOU THINK IT IS"

Shattering the Myths Behind the Misunderstanding.

R PHILLIP MITCHELL

authorHOUSE®

AuthorHouse™
1663 Liberty Drive
Bloomington, IN 47403
www.authorhouse.com
Phone: 1 (800) 839-8640

Published by AuthorHouse 10/09/2015

ISBN: 978-1-5049-5369-6 (sc)
ISBN: 978-1-5049-5370-2 (hc)
ISBN: 978-1-5049-5368-9 (e)

Library of Congress Control Number: 2015916067

Print information available on the last page.

This book is printed on acid-free paper.

Contents

Dedication

This book is dedicated to all of the hurting, misunderstood and disenfranchised of our world.

Help is on the way!

Secondly, to all of those unnamed people who have supported me throughout the years, thank you!

When we are challenged by those in our lives who cause us to look inwardly, we are more likely to unearth treasures far beyond our wildest dreams.

Lastly, this book is dedicated to those who have paid the ultimate price, before the much needed help arrived. I hope you found your way.

Preface

I asked myself, what could I have done differently to make a significant difference?

After twenty plus years of visiting and revisiting this issue, this book was born.

Being able to see from many different perspectives will cause us to understand some of the concerns of others.

In turn, we could as a result, have a healthier overall attitude towards issues we may not be familiar with.

I trust you will indeed, never forget this journey.

Homosexuality; It's not what you think it is.

Shattering the myths behind the misunderstanding!

An intense study and forensic look into human sexuality, and its effects on us all.

2nd revised edition

R Phillip Mitchell

8/10/2015

Introduction

This book is not being written to confirm nor dispel any belief in the topic.

The writer's intent is to provoke the thoughts of the reader concerning this subject matter. One must admit, we have all been affected in one way or another.

The subject of sex is always a topic of taboo, because of new discoveries and many myths being unveiled.

Daily we grow in knowledge and our societies are ever expanding. As a result, we embrace trends new and old as well as seek out new interests with regards to relationships. In every Nation around the globe, this is true.

Homosexuality is a subject that has flustered scientists, theologians, philosophers, counselors, educators, clinicians and more.

Today, although more accepted than any time in history, questions remain.

There are old and new frontiers to conquer, and many new issues to understand concerning this classification.

In times past, laws were made to banish and punish those that engaged in any sexual activity with the same sex.

Today laws are vastly being passed on behalf of individuals and groups seeking fairness concerning their collective human rights, such as medical attention, protection of assets, wealth and that of free speech. The argument is however far greater than the surface issues we've heard and seen on many occasions.

Within the pages of this book, we will touch on many sensitive societal concerns regarding sexual orientation, sexual preference, and public perception.

In addition to, sharing several brief personal stories of real accounts of persons affected directly and indirectly by their experience and life challenges faced in this area.

It is of utmost importance for the reader to be completely open-minded. You may find information in this book enlightening and quite useful for daily living.

"A mind that is closed will never be open to new understanding."

If your endeavor is to understand more precisely the lifestyle and choices of those faced with the daily challenge of finding their true self within their sexuality, you've chosen the right reading material.

It is, however, important to read this work with a clear mind, rather than a critical viewpoint. Now let's take a life-changing journey into the topic.

"Homosexuality, it's not what you think it is."

The First Modern Trial

In 1772 Captain, Robert Jones was on trial, charged with sodomizing a thirteen-year-old young boy.

His argument was that the act was consensual, but at that time the age of consent was 14. As a result, Captain Jones was found guilty and eventually sentenced to die.

His trial drew much attention as people from all walks of life were outraged. Despite the apparent dissension and a public outcry, the case received consideration by the Royal seat of England.

To everyone's amazement, Jones received a full Royal pardon, but was ordered to leave the country to quell the disgust of the general public.

Many criticized England's government for its decision. As a result, the topic of same-sex prevailed in newspapers, behind closed doors and in the political arena.

There were protests demanding new laws governing and making the sexual conduct of any sort, illegal between parties of the same sex. In addition to, sodomy among any party male or female.

Captain Jones was extremely popular; he had a good legal defense team who was able to show the weakness of the evidence of his accusers, this had significant bearing on his pardon.

In the end, there arose tremendous objection from within the walls of Christianity as well as many political, scientific and theological circles. They questioned the morality of such acts and cited the absence of public acceptance.

No other issue at the time stirred up more heated debates from opposing proponents.

The basis of which became the driving force for future change, being looked upon as insidious to the future of any thriving community.

Open debates created platforms for many future activists who left their mark on history starting in 1869 in Austria.

Where did the term HOMOSEXUALITY come from?

Karl-Maria Kertbeny was born on February 28th, 1824 in Vienna Austria. Most noted for being a journalist, memoirist and most of all a human rights activist and campaigner.

Karl Kertbeny is famous for having coined the phrase **"Homosexuality."**

He worked closely with some of Hungary's notable poets and writers. As a profession, he was charged with translating their works into German.

Kertbeny became ignited on the subject of homosexuality by the plight of a close friend of his who happened to be homosexual.

After being blackmailed by someone trying to extort money from him, Karl's friend took his life not being able to handle the pressure from the potential public humiliation.

Noted for writing some twenty-five books on a host of subjects, Karl relocated to Berlin in 1868.

He remained single focused on his writings while being accused and sometimes questioned about his marital status. Some skeptics suggested that he was drawn to the liking of the company of other men.

Karl never gave these accusations any energy, refusing to answer any questions about his sexual orientation.

Shortly after, Karl devoted an extensive amount of his writing time towards the topic of homosexuality. When asked why he did this, he replied by saying he was inspired by "anthropological relevance."

In this, he was alluding to his sense of concern with respect to justice and the personal rights of every man.

"The Medical Model of Alternative Lifestyles"

Kertbeny implied in his writings; that homosexuality was inborn, and as a result, could not be altered. This statement became the basis of what we know today as the **"medical model "of alternative lifestyles and homosexuality.** He further contended that the Prussian sodomy law was a violation of person's rights.

His argument was; consensual sexual acts committed while in the privacy of one's home should not be looked upon as a criminal act and thus, subject to the law.

Being motivated by what happened to his friend, he argued concerning the plight of many who were driven towards suicide because Prussian law did nothing to blackmailers, who consistently extorted money from these types of individuals.

The prevailing argument of the day was; men committed acts of sodomy because they were just evil.

Kertbeny responded by bringing attention to the fact that many of the great heroes of human history were in fact themselves homosexual.

Being the first to put forth such strong and piercing statements caused much prejudice and provoked debates concerning the formation of words used to describe persons of this classification.

Thus, Kertbeny coined the word "**homosexuality**" in 1869. As a result, the words "**sodomite and pederast**" were abolished. He subsequently called the relationship between male and female "**heterosexualism**" and those that practiced anal intercourse "**pygists.**"

Soon after these and other writings little was heard from Kertbeny. His terms "homosexuality" and "heterosexual" were used widely by other noted sexual researchers. He lived to the age of fifty-eight dying in Budapest in 1882.

Today these words are common and are the terms most suited when talking or writing about the subject of sexual orientation.

Kertbeny is a respected figure in the history of the Hungarian gay community.

He is remembered for his painstaking and controversial work as he stood up for justice and equality for all homosexual persons.

Lastly, during the yearly gay festival, a new reef is placed upon his burial site.

Homosexuality, in the motherland "AFRICA"

Again, it is the sincere desire of the author to be extremely sensitive during the writing of this subject. My aim is the establishment of many platforms that will lead towards forensic discussion and observation.

Culture and sexuality have played a major part in the formulation of practices that makes each community unique.

In modern day society, we are sometimes ignorant concerning the effect of ancient and thus forgotten practices that have prevailed although altered, standing the test of time.

Several tribes in Africa practiced same-sex relationships; it was customary even among married persons.

"Understanding Intercrural sex, also known as femoral sexual intercourse."

Male partners were known to place their penis between the lubricated thighs of a partner, at which time he would thrust himself forward creating friction. The other action was the thrusting of the penis into the mouth and throat of one's partner.

Interfemoral sex is the act of placing one's penis on the abdomen of two partners and thrusting one's body back and forward.

Interfemoral sex was a practice of the Azande or Sandeh a cannibalistic tribe of the Congo in the 19th and 20th century.

Historians claim that same-sex marriages have been a matter of documentation in many countries outside the influence of Christianity for thousands of years.

It is said; one member of the union would decide to take on the role of the woman with all of the responsibilities of a female in a relationship with a male.

Being looked upon as women to the other tribal members, these persons choosing such roles would enter into the marriage being called spirit men.

Men wishing to marry these individuals were able to choose partners from early as twelve to upwards of twenty years of age.

They in turn would pay booty to the father of the young man, in exchange for his hand in marriage. Also, note these unions were temporary in nature.

However, these practices were, in fact, abolished, upon the settling of the Europeans in early 20th century.

Sexuality of African women

The Lesotho women were known to have long standing intimate unions with other women within their communities. These relationships were called **"motsoalle"** and were deemed socially acceptable.

Many husbands who worked in jobs far away encouraged their wives to enter into these relationships; not wanting them to be alone while they were unable to be by their side.

These unions were often preceded by a community affair, with ceremonies where there would be celebration consisting of the slaughtering of animals, eating, drinking, dancing and the sharing and exchanging of gifts.

This custom was also abolished and although remembered, seems to no longer be publically practiced and neither is it deemed socially acceptable.

Sexual practices of early Grecians

"Pederasty" was the most common form of same-sex relationships between males in tribal prehistory Greece, also known as **"Paiderastia"** which means "boy love."

In these unions, older men from about the age of 30 would seek out a young lover about 12 years old.

It was Grecian custom for such relationships to serve as a foundation for mentoring, courtship and in preparing the young man for life as an adult.

The older male was considered the figure of authority and as a result, would be the penetrating party of the relationship.

These individuals were considered role models. They provided love, protection and education for the young man.

Also, they were taught Grecian life and customs, and their responsibilities as adults until about the age of 17.

Pubic hairs made these boys unattractive and thus no longer desirable;

At that point, he was released from his relationship. Having gone through his rite of passage into Grecian society, now he was considered a man.

Greece had an enormous impact on the rest of the world including the Roman Empire; hence, many of its ideas concerning sexuality were embraced.

Subsequently, Greece had significant bearing on the views and customs of all ancient societies.

SOCRATES

Named among those who lived a homosexual lifestyle in Grecian society, are **Socrates** who lived between 469 BC–399 BC and **Plato.**

Socrates was a Greek philosopher and recognized as one of the founders of Western philosophy. Strikingly, he was also known for his contribution towards the field of ethics.

Today, Socrates theories are commonly used in a broad range of discussions.

He also made considerable contributions in the areas of epistemology and logic.

The end of his life was tragic. His views on Athenian politics came under close fire and as a result, he was brought to trial. After which, he was jailed and according to many historians, unjustly put to death.

PLATO

Plato lived between 428/427 BC –348/347 BC. A Greek philosopher, writer, and mathematician and is known for founding the first institution of higher learning in the western world. The organization is called the Academy, located in Athens Greece.

Plato was a faithful student of Socrates and as a result, much of his philosophy, thinking and writings were greatly influenced by his mentor and teacher.

Plato in one of his writings known as the Apology of Socrates stated that he indeed was devoted to Socrates.

Socrates was noted as pointing out Plato's name when mentioning him as one young man who was very close to him, hinting that he may have been corrupted by their relationship.

Ancient terms used to describe homosexual relationships in different cultures

Lady-boy- This term was widely used to describe young male lovers taken in early Eastern Asia by men and Royalty within these societies.

Kings of the time were known to have both male and female partners. Upon the settling of the Europeans, this practice was abolished.

Two-Spirit- this term was used among the indigenous people of the Americas before the Europeans colonized it.

These persons were set aside at very young ages and may have been born with both male and female genitals.

The parents of these children had a choice to raise them as either male or female.

After the decision had been made, they began teaching the child the ways of the gender that had been chosen.

Also, they were looked upon as having magical powers often being called shamans; persons with the ability to communicate with the spirit world.

There are those who perceive this as a threat, while others call it a form of homophobia that causes people to shriek.

They believe their whole lives may be altered by the mere thought of things changing.

These occurrences mentioned above have a most profound effect on all of us, our families our children and our future.

Today there is a sense of hush within the atmosphere as if to say, you do your thing and I'll do mine.

There must be constructive dialog that causes us to be authentic as we deal with these issues and many more not mentioned.

Today some parents are fighting to keep certain books out of their children's school.

These writings depict and teach that homosexual lifestyles are a part of everyday life, and it is altogether a matter of one's preference.

I thought school was a place to prepare children and others for the challenges and necessary matriculations of life, giving them all they need to succeed.

No one can disagree, every parent has a right to determine what is acceptable for their under-aged children to learn.

Let's keep in mind, in a day where a young child could be emancipated from his parents; the argument becomes harder to define.

The fact of the matter is, many parents who are trying to shield their children from the exposure to the knowledge or activities of a homosexual lifestyle are far too late.

Today television, movies, commercials, cartoons, family members, acquaintances, friends and peer pressure are working full time contending for the attention of these young and impressionable minds.

Only an ignorant parent believes he or she can totally shield their child without properly exposing and educating that child concerning particular issues of life.

One way or the other the child will be exposed, better at home in a controlled loving environment than in a place of much obscurity and misunderstanding.

A student confided in me one day saying, quote: my mom never wanted me to have anything to do with boys, so she sheltered and watched me closely all through my schooling.

Subsequently, she decided to send me to an all-girls' high school, to me it was like throwing me out of the frying pan into the fire, end quote.

This student described how she found an outlet for her sexual expression, being exposed to "the life" by her female peers whose parents may have thought the way her mom did.

If her mother would not have been ignorant about the phenomenon of all boys and girls schools and the pressures associated with such an environment, would she have changed her mind? We will never know.

"Making life altering decisions, without the consideration of proper information, can sometimes lead to devastating results."

True confessions from a young man entitled "He was my uncle."

"Dear Diary"

Dear diary I am tired of feelings of loneliness and insecurity going from home to home. I often wondered; **did anyone love me?** I remember screaming out in the dark of night, "**Daddy where are you!**"

It is funny I can still feel the sadness as I look out the window of my bedroom, into the playground across the street.

I can see some of the little boys of the neighborhood playing catch with their dads.

The question still lingers "**Daddy where are you?**" As my mind begins to play tricks on me, I am wondering was I the product of a one-night stand, or maybe I was just a mistake?

To this day, I don't know if I was displaced or misplaced.

In the midst of other children being born into my family, I seemed to have somehow gotten lost in the shuffle, always playing by myself.

Often, I pretended I was mom and dad, and my sister's dolls were the children.

Thinking, if I couldn't be happy; I would at least pretend I was as often and as long as possible.

One thing I now realize is, **as a child you never know who's watching you.**

Most of my friends growing up were female; I just felt un-intimidated in their presence. All the while I was carefully monitored by my uncle, who at that time was just released from prison.

Daily as I came home from school he greeted me at the front door. He always seemed strange to me, **but he was still my uncle.**

One night I found myself being afraid to sleep in my room alone and subsequently, he offered his bed to me. I saw nothing wrong with this; **he was my uncle.**

That very night, he pursued and violated me as a hungry lion after his helpless prey. He battered my fragile body taking advantage of all my innocence, as he turned my world inside out.

My uncle sexually abused me for many years. I never said a word.

I was afraid and somehow felt as though I had done something to deserve this treatment.

I felt sorry for my uncle as he continued using his charm, making me feel guilty each time he destroyed who I was inside.

Often I wondered, **would that have happened if my daddy were there?**

Grandma never suspected anything. Every time the doors of the church would open, grandma and I were there.

You can just imagine what was going through my head. I would listen attentively as the preacher preached, watching the people as they confirmed his every word by shouting Amen! Clapping with jubilation;

So many people loved my pastor. I constantly had dreams of how my life would have turned out if he were my father.

Grandma was the mother of the Church and of course, her favorite grandson "me" got all of the attention as a result.

By the age of 12 I began winning many awards for piano recitals and was somewhat proficient with computers.

My secret life at home led me towards pushing myself to do anything to forget what was going on inside, besides I enjoyed the attention I got from all I did.

Nothing grandma or the pastor taught me, could have prepared me for what was next.

One day I found myself going to Church to meet the minister of music for a brief rehearsal. As I arrived, I sat at the piano and began playing a song I wrote being all alone.

Moments later, the minister entered in and hovered over me as if to assist with my playing.

The next thing I knew, I was once again being violated, by someone I trusted, the minister of music.

To make matters worse, it happened in the Church the place where I once felt so secure.

What was I to do now? I thought maybe this was how it was meant to be. I had thoughts of dying and even taking my life that led to several attempts.

As I lay in the hospital about to lose my mind, I felt as though I brought this on myself.

Who can I tell, or would anyone believe me?

Everyone who visited me wished me well.

Grandma and the pastor prayed for me, yet no one knew what I was battling; doesn't that beat all, never the less my life goes on.

High school was a place of awakening for me. For the first time, I found myself now being attracted to other boys.

What in the world was I to do with this newfound feeling? No one would have ever imagined what was going on inside of me.

I've learned over the years how to use my shy, withdrawn demeanor to get people just to leave me alone. It felt so weird trying my hardest to be a boy, yet going through so many female tendencies.

I wanted nothing to do with men, yet I wanted them. Where do I go from here?

As time went on, I made many friends and became somewhat popular. I still attended the same Church as though everything was all right.

Upon becoming more mature and outgoing, to my surprise, I began attracting the attention of men (**closet homosexuals**) almost everywhere I went.

For the first time in my life, I openly admitted to being homosexual.

Since then my life has been plagued with one affair after another.

I am still entangled in the clutches of this lifestyle. Now I have a desire to be free, I hope it's not too late?

Sign:
Will.

Did Will, have a choice?

Although there are a great many claims of bliss and happiness by some who live the life of bisexuality or homosexuality, we can plainly see the effect of the encounter upon this young man's life.

We can only speculate that his uncle most likely was exposed to homosexual relationships while being incarcerated.

Could he not control himself when looking at his young nephew whom he was supposed to protect?

"When true love is present, there is a measure of restraint and respect that comes along with it."

Apparently, his lustful inhibitions could not be controlled as he sought an outward expression of his secret desire.

Now this young man's life has been entirely altered by his first sexual experience being with another man against his will.

Will's feelings had nothing to do with feelings from birth or an unbalance of hormones as some state.

Clearly, this was as a result of exposure to someone that took control of his innocence and nature.

Ultimately, he was afflicted with confusing thoughts that eventually led him to a lifestyle and desire for homosexual relationships.

Where were the protections that every child should enjoy?

The real question is, how many more innocent children were turned into victims by this predator?

I can see him lurking through the neighborhoods early in the morning as all the children are going to school, and watching as they play outside without the constant supervision of parents or adults.

Will said it all too well.

"As a child you never know who's watching you."

Daddy Where Are You?

None of us correctly handles all of the things that happened to us as we were growing up,

In due course, we each can decide to take control over whatever may have plagued us along the way.

How would you respond to Will?

Incest happens to be one of the leading causes of the initiation into alternative lifestyles. Coming in a close second is a personal acquaintance.

More times than any people are violated by those they know. Where were those who were supposed to be on the side of Will?

Moreover, as he asked so many times, where was his father?

It seemed as though those around him were so preoccupied with their lives that they did not realize he was always silently screaming out for help.

All across America and the world there are countless Wills, just another name, just another time, just another place.

How do you heal the scars left by the violent hands of a predator? On the contrary, we can choose to look the other way and put all of the blame on Will and people like him without ever trying to understand their struggle.

Coming Out Of the Closet

The world has been quiet for so long, finally one day those in the closet decided it was time to come out. They came out seeking more room to express themselves in search of relationships and remedies they believed were long overdue.

As for Will's grandma, she would have been devastated if she knew the truth. Never in a million years would she think, **her son was raping her grandson.**

The truth is, there are countless families who have hidden these types of secrets from one another and the public in an attempt to keep the family name.

We may never know the real impact of such behavior on the quality of life of many within our societies.

Now we see the issues arising on every front, and many are frantically trying to find answers to what should have been addressed months, years, decades and even generations ago.

"A House Void of Constant Maintenance, Will One Day Cause Those Inside To No Longer Be Protected By the Lingering Security of Its Deteriorating Walls"

Can you tell the difference?

Too often than not, we find people with a complex of avoidance as they believe, "that could never happen to me."

It is these very same individuals that are often unprepared for the unsuspecting challenge right around the corner.

Our world has drastically changed to the degree that homosexuals and lesbians work and play in every area of society, even if you do not know they are there, they are.

It's time to **stop fooling yourself as though you can tell the difference by mere outward appearance.**

From the neighborhood house; to the White House; to the courts of Castles and the aisles of Congress; to the poor house and the Mansion on the hill the Vatican and more.

Homosexuality is here!

Choose not to keep an old school mindset that refuses to study what's going on today.

Otherwise, you will be like the travelers of old who were afraid to go too far out in the ocean, fearing they would fall off the edge of the earth.

They thought the earth was flat when it was round; because of this fear they were robbed of the greatest journeys of their adventurous lives.

"Learning enhances wisdom and broadens the foundation from which it is launched."

"Fear is to the foolish man, a sidekick invariably leading to a place of no fulfillment."

Don't ask don't tell!

Today was not one of my good days. I found myself after twenty-six years telling my oldest son, the man he thought was his father really was not.

Needless to say, this was a very hard decision for me. All I could think of is what would ever happen if he found out by himself. I figured I had to take the plunge at some point in his life, why not now?

It all seemed so unfair lying to my son, as though I were protecting him. I came to the conclusion: he deserved to know the truth, I am tired and refuse to live with the guilt and fear anymore.

Being a single mother with three children was not always easy. My two boys demanded so much from me. I never expected to have to raise them all by myself.

I had no preparation. I just had to buckle up and go for it. Besides, as a mother all I wanted was the best for my children.

There is one thing I need to get off my chest. I am a minister at the neighborhood Church, and I don't know how I'm going to help anyone if I don't get some help for myself. Besides, it is time to come clean. It's now or never.

For years, I've been trying to reach out to my son Ken who always needed more attention than his other siblings.

It seemed as though he was affected by my being abused by his father when he was younger. I went the extra mile for Ken trying everything, and nothing appeared to work.

Where have I gone wrong? Recently, I found out that he may have had an inappropriate relationship with another boy who lives just next door.

I tried talking to him; but he is so angry with me, he will not let me get close to the subject.

Am I to blame for his life being what it is?

When Ken was 15, we lived in Tennessee in a quaint little community near Ft Campbell Army base. There were many men in our neighborhood, most of whom were all active and retired soldiers.

I worked late most nights and was always concerned for the kids. My other two, Jenny and Max, gave me virtually no trouble at all.

Ken challenged me on every end. As a result, finding something of interest for him to do seemed to be leading from one dead end to another.

Months went by, and one day as I was enjoying a day off, I decided to take a walk alone through the neighborhood.

While heading back home, I met the most wonderful man named Jim. He lived several doors away.

We began chatting and became friends. Although we both were single, we never were more than friends.

He was divorced and had two grown children and several very energetic grandchildren.

It seemed as though we always talked about our kids. A few months after meeting Jim, Ken turned sixteen. As a result, I asked Jim if he would be a much needed mentor for Ken. He was elated at the idea.

They began spending vast amounts of time together, and boy was I happy to see Ken enjoy himself with his new friend and father figure.

Jim enjoyed play sports and was pretty outgoing; he loved camping, fishing and doing things around the house. Ken jumped right in and never missed a beat.

I was amazed at his remarkable change. Then two years later we moved away, and of course Ken took it pretty hard. He began staying to himself quite a bit.

Realizing he missed Jim, I decided to allow him to visit him for the entire summer vacation each year.

Ken and Jim kept in contact for three years after we moved. The phone buzzed one Sunday morning as we were getting ready for Church.

One of our old neighbors told us Jim had suffered a massive heart attack the night before and didn't make it.

I did not know how to break the news to Ken, but somehow I mustered up the strength, and as I broke the news to Ken he began to sob violently.

I shouted "Lord I need you now" I held on to my child and began rocking him in my arms as though he were just born.

I realized Ken had lost his best friend.

Now as I sit here telling you all these dramatic things I've been through, I feel stupid and betrayed.

Can you believe? When I broke the news to Ken about his real father, he broke the news to me about he and Jim being lovers.

My jaw dropped not knowing, what to say or feel. I thought to myself, Jim the man I trusted with the care of my son, is the very one who first touched him and exposed him to this lifestyle.

Ken went on to say, "Mom we were lovers since I was 16." If only I had known. My head began to hurt instantaneously. I was angry. How could this man have done this to my son all of these years without my noticing?

Now I am left with this unanswered question, how can I help my child?

I Trust you, but I don't know you?

Is it possible to trust someone you do not know? Blind faith is a very dangerous thing.

It is always difficult when it seems as though we find ourselves being blind-sided by situations in life that never give us any warning signs.

Are we just too busy to see them, or do we just make ourselves believe something other than what is there? I've learned to be always prepared for the unexpected by living upon a simple principal.

"Prepare for the worst, but expect the best."

Dealing with Crisis

Allowing yourself to become increasingly tempered after every blow you received from your challenges and life's experiences is crucial.

You must understand that progress brings opposition that is resistance, and every situation comes as a teacher.

Never give up or give in to the pressure because failure is not an option. Patience and persistence are character traits or distinctions necessary to ensure success. This is not the avoidance of a crisis but the ability to stand strong in the midst of it all.

At times we tend to be too hard on ourselves, and as a result we become ineffective in our strategies. Being too close to a situation can be catastrophic, which often leads to a short sighted or distorted vision.

"Success is not the avoidance of a crisis but the ability to stand strong in the midst of it all."

A New Perspective

Decide to step back or even step out of the situation and get a whole new perspective. As you begin reevaluating, seek to find how you can be most practical and helpful.

Secondly, ask yourself what would you have done differently had you known. Lastly, make a counter-plan of attack. There is a lesson in every storm of life.

Your strategy can be direct or indirect, passive or aggressive. Choosing the right method is vital. Bridge the gap between what you know now and what you did not know then.

Having an ear to hear is crucial. Listen more, speak less, and always remain ready to respond rather than react.

Proper communication is vital. HEAR MORE, SPEAK LESS.

Many times we miss warning signs because we just get tired of actually listening, not just to words but body language, attitudes, mood swings and more. Remember,

"WHERE THERE IS NO COMMUNICATION, THERE IS NO RELATIONSHIP"

The four essential components of a Healthy, Nontoxic relationship

1. Love 2. Honesty 3. Respect 4. Trust

Love: love is the one distinction or component of a relationship that is invaluable. A relationship void of this element will eventually find itself in peril. It embodies the composition of the other components noted above.

It is like an excellent recipe that is complete with the best of ingredients and void of nothing essential. Love sustains, love, endures, love is full of compassion, love forgives, love heals, love compels, love embraces truth, and True Love Never Fails.

Honesty

1. Honesty is the product of being both truthful and transparent.
2. It is knowing you've been open and honest towards the other party or parties and most of all, yourself.
3. Honesty says this is who I am; this is how I feel and this is what I have done. Honesty tells the history of a person with compassion, clarity and understanding.
4. Lastly, honesty compels one towards being truthful and authentic.

Respect

A significant attribute of respect is "**common courtesy**" It brings you to a place of understanding that everyone has boundaries that we each need permission to enter.

1. Respect extends common courtesy without fail.
2. Respect will not defame another or seek to embarrass, but rather aims to uphold the integrity of another.
3. Lastly, respect gives what it in turn expects to receive.

Trust

Trust is last because it is the one component that takes the longest to develop in a personal relationship.

You can love, be honest and respect someone you do not entirely trust. Seems ironic, but it is true. Trust is developed over time being spent with someone, going through trials and challenges together.

Trust says "**I've got your back.**" You will never put your life in the hands of someone you do not trust. Confidence is what makes someone say "what's mine is yours, and vice versa." Lastly, you will never trust someone you do not know.

Therefore, trust is reserved for those you know, or those who have proven themselves in being able to get the job done, and having a genuine vested interest in who you are and what you do.

For example, you don't have to know a fireman to trust that he knows how to put out a fire. You believe his ability because you know he's been trained in this area.

Seek to learn, live and implement these four components in your relationships.

Undoubtedly, it will lead you towards healthy, holistic and loving unions with people that understand the real essence of relationships between human beings.

Androgyny and the (LGBT) Community

There is a phenomenon within Society that has caused us to look at the issue of homosexuality in a different way.

This phenomenon is call "**Intersexed**" sometimes called male or female androgyny, or the term hermaphrodite. Medical experts have reported that yearly, between one and three babies out of every 1500 to 2000 are born with some intersex issue.

Today those classified as such prefer to be called intersexed persons rather than hermaphrodite. They live life being born with both male and female genitalia.

Androgyny is often used to describe a person who wears clothing that is not gender specific in addition to being intersexed. Such persons lead ordinary lives often until the question arises, **are you male or female?**

There is a great deal of misunderstanding in this area. As a result, many lives have been ruined while family members and the intersexed often face ridicule and alienation when trying just to live normal lives.

Would you consider an intersex person homosexual? If your answer was yes, then you are part of a growing number of ill-informed individuals who do not understand the struggles associated with living life as an intersex person.

They made the wrong choice

I heard a story of a very handsome young man, born intersex. His parents decided at birth that they would raise him as a female, teaching him all of the things a little girl should know.

All was well until puberty, when he began to grow breasts. He was so traumatized that he took a knife to his chest in hopes of removing this unwanted arrival.

He never told his parents that he felt like a boy all along, although having a vagina as well as a penis.

Upon becoming a young adult, he took matters into his hand. He pursued his role as a male, in spite of his daily challenges.

Eventually, this young man had to undergo extensive therapy for many years and continues even today.

He had no say in his upbringing, and no one bothered to ask him what he wanted to be.

They just assumed he would grow into their decision, and they proceeded towards fulfilling their dream of having a precious little girl.

The LGBT "Lesbian, Gay, Bisexual, and Transgender." This community had no problem embracing inter-sexed persons.

As a result, they have been welcomed and embraced with open arms, thus strengthening their arguments and overall position in society.

A star is born

Jean C, A famous world record holder was born in the early 1900's. She started running seriously at the age of 12, and never looked back. She is noted for being World, junior and Olympic champion in the 800-meter race and more.

This young woman garnered the attention of the sporting world as she became a spectacular athlete and a feared adversary at the same time.

Amidst her many victories great curiosities arose concerning her athletic ability; and as a result, speculation grew among her peers regarding the possibility of steroid use and also talks about her possibly being male.

She allegedly came under attack from the Athletics Association who ordered testing for performance enhancing drugs in addition to gender testing.

This news had broken only hours before she was scheduled to run in the World Championships.

Although winning once again, Jean was so distraught about the turn of events that she thought about boycotting the medal ceremony.

Not only was she under constant worldwide scrutiny, her name, records and all she had worked hard for were all in jeopardy of being tarnished and potentially taken away.

After testing and many months of waiting, Jean was completely exonerated; she was found to be inter-sexed from birth and, as a result, could legally and naturally embrace womanhood.

She and her family are said to be members of Lion Christian Church in her native land where she resides and is respected and celebrated among her nation's people.

Young but Not Innocent

I met a young boy today; he was 16 to be exact, very intelligent, strikingly good-looking and extremely well mannered. He must have good parents I thought. With my next observation, I noticed he acted extremely feminine by the way he walked and moved his hands.

I asked myself, what could have gone wrong with this child?

He stood next to my wife as a client sat in her chair. Then he uttered, "Can you show me how to do hair like that Mrs. D?"

I sat down in silence mesmerized with his persistence and unashamed demeanor.

Later I found out, he asked my wife for a job in the salon. I whispered, "Isn't he too young to work here, babe?" Waiting for an answer, she smiled as she turned her head saying, "No he is not."

We wasted no time discussing the fact that he was open about his sexual preference and as a result, how the customers might react.

After much thought and consideration, we decided to give him a chance, thinking maybe this would open a door for us to help him.

In the beginning, he only did manicures and pedicures. I let him do my nails a few times; He was superb and passionate about his work.

By the way, his name is Jay. Every time he saw me he became excited and began to talk about his life as though I knew him forever.

I was surprised to find out his mother supported his every move. As time went on he began working full time in our Salon, no more room for school.

My wife and I thought, at least we were keeping him out of the streets. Soon after, Jay began testing our boundaries.

He started wearing extensions down his back, nails as long as claws and of course makeup, long lashes, blush, lipstick and more.

I tried talking to him to no avail. He thought it was funny. One day he'd do it, the next day he would not. Last week I came into the shop, and Jay shocked me as he shouted "Pastor is it all right if I come to Church in a dress?"

Being caught off guard, I yelled, "No it is not all right!" Shortly after that, my wife and I decided Jay was too much, and we had to let him go.

He left gracefully and within a week he had his very own salon, just down the street from our location. His clientele was unbelievable.

I could not believe a 16-year-old boy was single handily running his own salon.

Before long Jay was in the process of getting hormone shots and implants. By then he was 17 going on 30.

He became the talk of the town; this was exactly what Jay wanted.

Several months later Jay no longer looked like himself. As his new transformation began to take shape, he had breast implants, high cheek bones and hips like a woman.

As I passed by his shop one day, he proudly confessed he was about ready to begin his sex change. I wondered if this was legal or even possible for a person as young as Jay.

It seemed as though no amount of my reaching out had been of any benefit to Jay.

Never the less, I felt compelled to continue showing him that I cared, not knowing what tomorrow would bring.

The last day I saw Jay was Friday of last week. A pastor friend of mine was in town, and he needed some suits.

We proceeded to the suit shop next to Jay's. As we exited the vehicle, Jay came out to greet me and turned to my company blurting out "You're cute." I was embarrassed and speechless to say the least.

I continued all the while, ignoring Jay.

As we returned to my vehicle, my pastor friend turned towards me and said; "Those young girls are something else." I answered him with a smile on my face revealing to him the person he was referring to was a young boy.

Needless to say, he was shocked with utter amazement; we shrugged it off and went about our day.

The next day was gloomy, I woke up with a funny feeling in my gut, but I proceeded to do my morning devotion as usual.

After which, I decided to go fetch the newspaper and return home for some relaxation.

As I pulled into the driveway, one of the members of the Church pulled up yelling,

"Pastor Jackson, did you hear?" Hear what child, I replied. She let out a sigh and broke the news to me, suddenly saying.

Jay was found dead under the Second Street Bridge this morning. My heart was filled with sadness as my eyes filled with tears.

Later that day I was told, Jay had been picked up by a stranger who thought he was a woman. Upon finding out otherwise, the stranger responded violently and slit Jay's throat leaving him to bleed to death.

It is true; sometimes we want things for others that they do not wish for themselves. Still I press on with the memories of Jay. I know deep down inside of him, there was a child screaming out for help.

As you can see by my experience, **it is impossible to help everyone with what we do; but on the other hand you never know who will be helped by what you do.**

It is now two years later, and Jay is still the talk of the town.

Your Church cannot help Me!

Why is it that many pastors expect people to come to their Churches already fixed up? Isn't the Church a place where people are supposed to be able to come as they are, just raw, complicated and in need of guidance?

The Church seems to be the one place that traditionally has not been able to address the issue of Homosexuality and Lesbianism with an overall healthy outcome.

I believe if the bum on the street can come as he or she may be, shouldn't the same courtesy be extended to all aspects and facets of our societies?

For example, when I look at the hospital it is a place of healing for all. It's where no one is supposed to be discriminated against regardless of the person's plight.

In a hospital there are trained physicians and others who work together. They each tend to the ailments of those who walk in or are brought through their doors.

Their primary intent is to administer healing and to maintain an atmosphere of wellness for all. It is not merely the doctor making the patient well, but rather the patient and doctor working together for a solution best suited for total recovery of the patient.

The process of working towards a healthy outcome for the patient is the goal. The doctor must figure out what and where the problem is, and the symptoms associated with it.

Keep in mind, the problem is always deeper than what is seen on the outside.

Ultimately, the patient has to convey to the doctor the symptoms they are experiencing and what part of the body is being adversely affected.

Where do you come from and where have you been?

Knowledge of the family history is often essential when diagnosing the patient. Secondly, information about the person's daily activities is also viable in addition to any information about previous treatment received by that person.

In short, a proper forensic evaluation of the person's situation is necessary to begin rendering adequate remedies or solutions towards the wellness of the individual. I often wonder, what would happen if spiritual healing were approached in this way.

There must be an atmosphere of openness that compels those that come into our presence towards feeling comfortable, as they search inside themselves for the answers they are in need of.

Surrender yourself to the healing process.

The words we speak, and the life we live serve merely as a beacon of light, which is the answer for every dark situation.

Although you may be going through challenges, a tuff situation, an unfortunate circumstance, or a trial, you can and will make it. If you believe in what God has placed inside of you.

Don't give up, but rather GET UP!

Get up to fulfill the purpose for which you were born! There is something unique inside of you that cannot be duplicated by anyone; you are an original concept of the creator of the universe.

No matter how small or great, no one is insignificant!

Remember "Little is much when you put it in Creator's hand."

"PURPOSE WORKS LIFE"
Moreover, LIFE WORKS ON PURPOSE,
FIND YOUR PURPOSE YOU FIND YOUR LIFE

Isn't the goal of life to find one's purpose? **I honestly believe it is, not merely to find it but to fulfill it!** As we matriculate through school, I believe education does not come to teach us who we are, but rather it begins to make a demand on our God-given abilities.

In other words school comes to show you what you do not know, you already know. I will leave this explanation for another book.

The challenge comes when our children are exposed to conflicting information. They are then left to deal with this new demand for their attention concerning things they have not learned to process correctly.

In such cases, since young minds do not have the capacity to deal constructively with this new knowledge, they settle for the interpretation given to them.

It can be quite dangerous because miss- information or lack of adequate information in anything can lead to permanent injury to the mind, body, and spirit resulting, in some cases, death.

"THIS INFORMATION IS A MATTER
OF LIFE AND DEATH

The Principal Violation

Hello, my name is Phillip. Next week I'll be celebrating my 40th birthday, a significant milestone in my life.

My 8-year-old son came home today after school pretty elated about his good grades.

This day was no different from any other. We decided to sit down together so could tell me all about his accomplishments.

Soon after, he pulled out a lollipop with a proud look on his face and shouted "I can massage better than anyone in the class!" I was not sure what he meant by that; I stayed quiet as he rambled on in excitement.

"I got the lollipop for massaging my teacher's legs better than anyone else," he uttered.

Of course, I was in shock. After that, I gently proceeded explaining to my son how inappropriate this type of behavior was.

Thank goodness he completely understood me. As I began to ponder on the whole thing, I realized doing it was bad enough, but then rewarding him was a setup.

The Place called Stitt

Later on that night lying in bed, my wife being fast asleep, I began having thoughts of when I was a young boy in junior high school.

It was the summer of 1978 almost the end of the year; everyone was excited about the school trip to Great Adventures.

Many of my friends were upset about not being able to go, because their parents could not afford the $50.00 fee.

During recess, those of us not making the trip decided to enter the playground for a quick game of stickball; waiting to pass the time. Soon after the game was over, I reentered the school and proceeded down the hallway towards my classroom.

As I passed other homerooms, I noticed some of my friends leaving their classrooms one by one.

Moments later, Efrain approaches me stating, "Mr. Jacob would like to see you in his office." Mr. Jacob was at that time the assistant principal of our school.

Thinking I had done something wrong, I asked Tony if he knew why he wanted to see me. Efrain pulled me to the side and quietly whispers, "He wants to see if you need any money to help you go on the school trip." After that, he began explaining to me what he had just done in the Assistant Principals office.

Tony revealed to me that Mr. Jacob had a book with pictures of the different private parts of fellow students. He received an undisclosed sum of money for allowing his penis to be measured and photographed by Mr. Jacob.

Apparently he wanted me to join in as well. I became infuriated and disgusted.

47

I was upset with Tony and asked him why he thought I would do such a thing.

I said to myself, Mr. Jacob has lost his mind. I then told Tony I was going to get my bat, make my way to the office and wait for Mr. Jacob. My intention was to give him a taste of the wood from my brand new stickball bat.

Lucky for both of us, he stepped out for a few minutes; so I sat down outside the office waiting anxiously. I began visualizing hitting him with the bat as soon as he asked me to participate as my friends did.

Tony was afraid and came after me with several others. Eventually, they convinced me to return to the classroom fearing they would get in trouble as I exposed the situation.

For the rest of the day, they begged me not to tell anyone. As a result, I never revealed this incident, not knowing any better at the time, thinking I was protecting my friends.

There is no telling how many boys and girls have been violated by Mr. Jacob. He was married and had children of his own.

To this day, I wonder what would have happened if had I exposed this assistant principal's violation of his oath as an educator and his responsibility to the children attending my old school.

Twenty plus Years later, I am faced with this situation concerning my son. I cannot let this one get away; I'll be at his school first thing in the morning.

Prevention Is Better Than Cure

What is this world coming to?

Life as we know is full of predators of all types genders and professions. As mentioned before, these are individuals who prey on the weak and impressionable. And they are manipulators seeking to fulfill their sick desires.

They never once think of the possible permanent scarring and damage they are inflicting on their victims.

Could you even imagine what their lives may have been like growing up? All too often, it is the scenario of **the violated becoming the violator.**

"Where there is Prevention, a cure is never needed!"

Moving Violation!

Just think of how many parents and caregivers could have avoided the pain and embarrassment their children and families had to encounter, all because someone could not control an impulse.

We must begin to reach these potential violators before their uncontrollable urge to reach out and touch someone alters another life.

Often we spend too much time on one side of the fence, looking for all the victims we can round up, as we begin strategically injecting them with lethal doses of what they did wrong.

I must admit, we must do a better job equipping our children by teaching them the boundaries they must never cross or allow others to pass.

Keep in mind; iolators are usually experts in manipulation. They seek out needy individuals starved for affection, love, attention and more.

"Never allow your children to leave home in need."

"This is not a question of the material wealth of goods, but rather ethical and personal values."

The father in this true story depicted was only in Junior High school when he chose not to follow the lead of his friends.

Despite his parents not having the money to send him on the school trip, he chose to do the right thing. Unlike some, the lure of money did not convince him to move in their direction.

"Don't be afraid to teach them."

Take advantage of every opportunity you get to teach your children. I believe it is better to expose the lies by telling them the truth. Spoon feed it if you must; but please, don't hide it because you think your children are too young or might not understand.

Teach them according to the level they are on. I would rather be the one sharing with my child, rather than some stranger who might have ulterior motives. I trust you agree!

It is important to know, once your child has a life changing experience it sometimes latches on, burying itself deep within the individual, waiting until the opportune time to begin yielding the hidden forbidden fruit.

Don't let it happen. Now is the time to intercede on behalf of all of our precious little ones. Lift a standard and teach them how to **RESIST and just say NO!**

Damn, she left me for another woman?

I remember being in college on the football team. All the guys used to sit around after practice and just talk a bunch of junk. They bragged about all of their latest conquests and who was next blah, blah, blah.

Being the kind of person who never took a liking to all the confetti, I often sat off to the side. There was one guy named Rick who was on the verge of getting a record deal for his group.

I cannot name them because you would definitely know who they are (smile). He always came to me and would just talk about his life and the daily challenges he faced juggling school, football, and a budding musical career.

He was an interesting person with good information and conversation to offer.

This guy was liked by many females, because they knew he was in the music industry. Ultimately, he revealed he was already a faithfully married man.

Rick seemed to have it all together, until one day he came in pretty distraught and somewhat withdrawn.

Feeling some apprehension I got up the nerve to ask him what was going on; he turned towards me with bloodshot eyes and blurted out **"Damn, she left me for another woman."**

I remember my jaw hitting the floor as I held my composure. I responded by telling him the same lame thing we all say when we really don't know what to say: "It's going to be all right" Of course I lied.

After which, we both found a quiet spot to sit and talk. Rick was now battling in his mind as to his adequacy as a man.

He thought buying the gifts and going on trips and driving a nice car was enough to keep his relationship going strong.

He kept repeating, "How could she do this to me?" I think he may have handled it better if she had left him for another guy.

That day I realized there is another dynamic in relationships that leads some to walk away from perceived material comfort towards a search to fill hidden voids and test the bounds of their humanity.

"We all want it and need it, but there are some things money cannot buy."

An Angel Next Door

My son just got out of jail, and he won't even take a look at his daughter. He somehow seems not to understand her need to have him in her life.

I've raised her from the day of her birth. Her mother, unfortunately, wanted nothing to do with her, so she became my responsibility.

I thought I was through raising children, but it seems as though I was wrong. When I look at my granddaughter, I want nothing but the best for her.

Over the years, my life has been nothing but a tangled web of one bad relationship after another. I remember when I first got tired of being used and abused about 12 years ago.

I found myself in a deep state of depression, with nowhere to turn. I even went to Church religiously, but things grew worse as each day passed on.

Being tired of the relationship rollercoaster I became a loner, only going out with other women, friends from time to time; this was when I experienced my first endeavor into a relationship with another woman.

It all happened so fast. One evening after work, I decided to go to the neighborhood bar. I began drinking one round after another in a futile effort to drown all of my sorrows. Sitting right next to me was the most beautiful woman I had ever seen.

She noticed me staring at her and uttered "Is everything ok?" Moving closer, I began telling her about my situation with men and relationships and how unfair things have been.

To my surprise all of my words fell on attentive ears. She drew nearer, embracing me as I began weeping profusely. She then suggested we move over to a quiet seating area with a more intimate setting.

I was broken. She began consoling me by telling me just what I wanted to hear.

Her words still linger in my ear as I remember her soft sweet voice telling me how insensitive men are and how they just don't understand women.

I thought to myself, could I have finally found a friend that understood me? Now the table was turned. After all she listened to me; I figured the least I could do was to listen to her.

My last words were, "all I wanted was for someone to love me". She then whispered "No one knows how to make a woman feel good like another woman does."

It was as if I never heard the woman part. To my surprise at that moment, I found myself in the arms of another woman.

Twelve years later, and now I am a Grand-Mother, I still don't know what to do. The truth of the matter is that this other lifestyle did not help my circumstance any. It only pacified and complicated my situation.

For a while, all seemed well, but on the other hand, my life was full of ridicule. I hid from family and friends as if they did not know.

Now I am watching my grandbaby and wondering what her life is going to be like. Living like this is like being trapped in someone else's body.

Daily I am screaming from the top of my lungs, but no one hears me. As I look in the mirror, my face is fixed with a smile that seems permanent yet it is only a facade.

I believe God is there for me, yet I struggle while dealing with the hardest thing I've ever had to fight. Why do some people think leaving this lifestyle is like when one quits smoking or drinking? I wish it were that easy.

This craving has the tendency to torment the one it lives inside. Nothing feels right anymore. I don't even enjoy doing the unmentionable. Lately, I've just become numb.

Now while I suffer from depression and self-persecution, my desire to do right increases each day. I am learning to love God, and of course myself again.

Old thoughts still come, but I never yield to them. Daily, I find myself meditating more on what I need to do, to be there for my grandbaby. It is challenging, but I often wonder if I will ever be free again.

I thank God every night for his grace and mercy and also for my new next-door neighbor.

She is the mother of the Church I've been attending.

One night I was at my lowest and about to take my life. I had a few drinks and had put a fresh bullet in my revolver, determined to end my pain.

All of a sudden, I heard a knock on my door, and it was my next door neighbor, old mother, Jean. Putting my revolver away, I then opened the door to her smiling face and her motherly voice.

"Hello, honey" she said." I was thinking about you and decided to bake you a cake. Momma loves you.

I wonder what would have happened if she were like most Christians, never witnessing, no smiles, always keeping to themselves. If only Christians knew how important they are.

**Momma Jean saved my life, with a cake
and words of encouragement.**

After all, God used her to save my life. Now that I am on the way towards being totally free, my desire is to help someone else. Just remember this!

**You never know who's on their last straw.
You never know who's on the edge.
You never know who lives next door.
You never know whose life you might save.**

Just imagine not entertaining strangers. Could it be, the one you passed by today may have been a life you could have saved? All I know is; **God sent an Angel next door just for me.**

If I Knew Then, What I Know Now

If only we knew the countless times we've been unconsciously used to stop someone else's tragedy.

We are living in an age where almost everyone seems to be over-burdened and under-compensated in every area of their lives.

At times, it is as if you are living life trapped in a body that belongs to someone else. We must at all cost seek to regain control over those things we lost during our struggles by changing our perception of our experience.

If our angle of and about the incident could change just a bit, it will make a significant difference.

The incident "HAPPENED" and it no longer exists!

See the good; don't dwell on disappointments and situations that sap you of your motivation to move forward. Remember, our lives must reflect our purpose and be headed towards the divine idea for which we were created.

Many people give their pasts and their issues far too much credit, as though they are ever present with every breath they take.

Now, it is time to take control of your life, and
leave the fictitious baggage behind!

The only battles you lose are the ones you do not resist!

The art of subtlety is always used in
planting seeds of deception.

The truth of the matter is, what some say is the devil ends up
being their flesh, with its affections, inhabitations, and lust.

It is time to be transformed by renewing your mind daily.

You must begin to saturate yourself in positive,
holistic situations, praying consistently for
the answers that can only come from Divine
intervention, for your particular circumstances.

Be consistent in not allowing your focus to be broken.

There is a pattern you can follow to attain
real deliverance and transformation.

Others have been delivered; so can you!

God's purpose for your life is absolute.

Your past can in no way disqualify you from your God-given future. Stay on course. All of us can look back over our lives and remember when what we used to do didn't work anymore.

That is why living your life according to yesterday's shortfalls and accomplishments only leads to duplication of the past and more disappointments.

Grow up if you will, stop letting life dictate to you what your next move will be. Learn how to make decisions that will move you towards being committed to success.

Before long, without a doubt you will begin seeing yourself as the strong, beautiful person you are.

"Show me your friends, and I will show you your future."

Joy and Pain

I was 15 when I got pregnant with my son, and my mother was as strict as they come. Her daddy was a Pastor, and he kept her in Church all of her life. Needless to say, she was very disappointed in me. Mother did everything she could to keep me from the boys, but nothing worked.

After finding out I was pregnant, she turned into my personal warden. I was under lock and key and the only thing missing was a chastity belt. To make matters worse, mother stopped talking to me. She now only gave orders.

The father of my baby was one of the boys from school. I thought we were in love, but found out when he got what he wanted, all of that changed.

I hardly can remember being around any boys after he left me. He told me he loved me, and now everything momma said began registering.

"Boys are no good; they only want one thing, they don't love you, and what can he do for you?"

I turned to my girlfriends in Church and school. It is funny; parents are always on the lookout for the other sex, if they only knew.

My mother never taught me anything about sex. She always said, "Keep your skirt tail down, and keep your legs closed." The subject of sex was taboo in my house.

I began dibbling and dabbling in other ways of fulfilling the desires of my raging hormones. I am the type I'll try anything once. I like being in control and the power that comes with it, always looking for a challenge.

Growing up the boys had nothing on me. I distinctly remember them at lunch as they talked about the girls as if they were just puppets.

When they got tired of us, they would just throw us away. I felt I had to rescue my sisters from such unfair treatment. After all, I was one of the girls, or so I thought.

One day I found myself in the middle of a squabble over a seat in the lunchroom. Would you believe in the heat of the moment, the one I argued with called me a **"dyke"** which was a slap in the face? I suddenly realized maybe I was not one of the girls after all.

Deep within, I always harbored mixed feelings. Troubled by my early pregnancy, I began wearing boys clothing, trying to hide what I once flaunted.

Never once did I realize a transformation was taking place as I became more accepted by the boys. I endeavored to do everything they could do better.

This mission led me to a place of hidden desires and alternative lifestyles. Like the clothes, they fit me well.

Soon I was old enough to explore, going where I had never gone, and doing what I had never done.

Mother still has nothing to say, she just looks at me with a blank stare in her eyes. I like the way I am; besides, she dosen't know how I feel.

She says I am hurting her and my baby but somehow I just can't see that. I guess I was born to be this way. I am still attending Church, I sing, play drums and even read the scripture from time to time.

My thought is, if my Pastor does not say anything to me, why should she or anyone else?

That is what's wrong with Church folk, always wanting others to accept their opinion.

Besides, everybody needs something to keep them praying; maybe this is my inspiration?

Do you think I am going to change? For what, just to please you? Never in a million years. I told you I was happy being this way.

"There is a time and season for every purpose under the sun, even deliverance."

NEVER GIVE UP!

A parent's self-analysis

Where did I go wrong? A question sometimes left unanswered for many parents: How do you deal with a rebellious child you love dearly?

Incidentally, I found myself asking this same question as I stared aimlessly into my bedroom mirror. Do you remember how many times you found yourself afraid of touching the subject of your child's sexuality and hoping one day they would begin confiding in you?

Avoidance works for a while until that faithful day you start seeing more of what you do not understand and may be opposed to.

I denied for several years the sense I had that my child was gay. Trust was necessary for me. As a result, I worked hard on having a meaningful relationship with him. Everything was all right as long as we were dealing with other people's business.

Well, one day it all came crumbling down. Initially, I thought it was a sudden change until I began reflecting back on all of the signs I chose to ignore.

Deciding to confront my son with the question **"Are you a homosexual?"** That was one of the hardest things I ever had to do. After finding countless e-mails on the computer in his room, which included nude pictures of other young men, I felt utterly betrayed.

Thinking to myself, how could I have been so blind? Even after seeing earrings, eye and tongue piercings, hair coloring, and press-on nails. I talked myself into believing he was just going through a punk rock phase.

Little did I know, he was in all reality coming out. Now twenty-one, he began verbalizing his need to express himself more each day. Soon after he confessed to me, it was as if his attitude was "now you know; it is time to show." He began openly having homosexual relationships.

Next came his beginning to wear female attire. That is where I finally decided to draw the line. At some point, you've got to say enough is enough. I had to raise a standard in my house.

It was difficult having a young son at home watching his elder brother as he began openly expressing his sexuality. No longer did I feel safe leaving them alone.

After that, I forbade my son from wearing female attire or anything feminine in our home. Of course, he did not take this well. Next, he murmured "I thought you loved me."

If he could only realize, my love for him was genuine as could be. I just didn't love what he was doing with his life.

Like the girl in the story before, he thought his endeavors had nothing to do with his family. They believe as they state **"I am not hurting anyone."**

Nothing could be further from the truth!

We love you, and what you go through, we go through!

It really hurts

As long as I found myself counseling others in this area, I was all right. However, the day it became personal, I found myself digging deep within every area of my life for the answers to this new found challenge.

I must admit, at times I felt like giving up on my son. Now I had a personal experience that changed my perspective on life forever. Many parents wait far too long before confronting their children about matters of concern.

Don't wait for them to come to you, you go to them, with all of the love and questions you have inside.

So much has changed

I implore parents and others to learn as much as possible in hopes of help their children, and those they love. Much has changed, as the world we once knew has evolved right before our very eyes.

Always leave the door open for their return but never allow the standards of what is right to be torn down or compromised.

Don't be critical, be loving but firm. Compromising will only lead to more frustration on your part, and it will cause you to evade the piercing questions that may need to be addressed.

I do realize we cannot change the past, but we will have something to say about our future. Take a stand and begin to decree:

"Now I will be strong through every stage and challenge of my loved one's life."

Where Do We Go From Here?

There is a new coin being used to purchase so-called dreams and visions. The side containing heads reflects the image of people that make socially acceptable things they believe they do not have power over and thus, cannot change.

On the tails side, we see the inscription saying, "If we avoid it, we will not have to deal with it." Needless to say, this coin is counterfeit and is not legal tender.

Society and the Church must stand up and cease from their former position and expand their scope without endeavoring to quarantine certain types of individuals or socially unacceptable behavior they do not understand.

No one ignores an infection for long. Soon it demands your attention as it begins to affect and infect other parts of the body until something must be done.

There is, however, an atmosphere in which faith and hope can excel. It is where dreams are realized, and evidence is seen.

We must seek to find a common ground on which we can converse, thus creating potential situations for healing and restoration between all men, races, creeds, and distinctions.

"**Wholesome words can heal the souls of the bruised as they pierce the crevices of the halls of criticism, disdain and hopelessness within the hearts of the broken.**"

Alternatively, is it more important to be critical, rather than receptive and understanding towards the plight of another? Many fail to be helpful because they come with preexisting notions and beliefs that hinder the possibility of one reaching out towards their place of need.

The apprehension comes because the injured feel as though they are already dammed without a word ever being spoken.

At times like these, we must seek to engage and disqualify the fear that is present. It is important to work towards setting an environment where the possibility of healing, helping, consoling, understanding and confronting in a loving way is present.

Trust is a clear distinction that is necessary during these instances. When established, everyone involved will begin moving towards a place of healing.

I am different for a reason!

Because of being different, many people will experience criticism by those who are quick to judge. What causes people to be critical to the point of cruelty?

Are they somehow insecure or threatened while in the presence of certain kinds of individuals? It is true that we each have the right to live as we please, but what I am stating goes even further than this. My thought continues on the next page.

Here is a story that might explain my thought

I had a friend named Frank who bought his first home in a beautiful small town in the South. The neighborhood was historical in nature, 100 plus year old houses lined both sides of the street.

Giant oak trees could be seen all over the block; and while each home had something distinct about it, one could clearly see that there were many similarities.

My friend being excited about the purchase of his first house, set out to make it a home by doing some cleanup and adding some personal touches. On the list was to cut down some of the trees, put up some fencing, and to paint the outside of the house.

As he began, there was a great sense of excitement within the air. Day one, clean up all went well. Day two and three, trees to be cut back and a few to cut down.

Day four, five and six, time to install the new fencing to privatize the back yard and also the front.

The next week came along, and he began to prepare for the painting of the outside of his home. He began painting his home in the most beautiful baby blue color. His wife Marge had it custom mixed at the local home improvement store.

It seemed as though the neighbors were excited to see the dramatic change as he and his wife continued to work, pressing towards completing their goal.

The following day as they prepared to continue painting, a gentleman pulled up in a white vehicle and approached the home with a booklet in his hand.

"Good morning" he uttered as they replied the same He then introduced himself as the local code enforcement officer.

He then asked Frank, if he had a permit to do the work he had done. Frank responded by saying, "I did not think I needed a permit to cut my trees, put up a fence in my yard and paint my house."

The code enforcement officer explained to Frank that he was in violation of the county code and the neighborhood covenant. As a result, he had to issue a fine.

Frank did not know that he needed permission to cut the trees, put up a fence and paint his house a particular color.

Their excitement now turned into disappointment. They now understood why all of the homes in the neighborhood looked somewhat the same. It was because of the historical covenants that governed what could and could not be done to each property.

They owned it, but they needed permission to make changes to the home. Not knowing cost Frank and Marge about 3000 dollars in expenses they could have avoided had they only known.

Well it is all right now, the last I heard Frank and Marge finally settled all of the issues, and their new house is now a home.

It can be said, looking at Frank and his wife Marge's situation that this is the way that many have been approached concerning their differences.

Once it becomes offensive to us, we want to penalize them as if to say you are bringing down my property value!

Our value increases when we become the type of person that can be counted on to help others in situations that may not seem favorable or healthy.

On the other hand, many don't want to be seen with certain kinds of people for fear of society's perception of them being tainted or tarnished.

Can you imagine passing by a dumpster and as a result, it causes you to begin smelling like the trash within?

Thank goodness it does not happen that way.

If this were the case, then the real question would be: Who's more trashy, the one with the problem? Or the one who can help but refuses to help? Can we call this pride or ignorance?

Is it Love or Lust?

Homosexuality is defined as a sexual relationship between two or more persons of the same sex. I've counseled many individuals who were totally against this interpretation.

Some honestly believe they are in love.

Is it rather lust, instead of love? I often questioned saying "If you love them and you say it is not about the sex, why then include sex?" I never got an answer, except **"I don't know."**

Lust is a spirit that plays on one's weakness, vulnerability, and natural desires. It always leads those caught in its clutches towards a web of deception, After that, it takes them on a ride aboard life's emotional roller coaster.

When it is finished, these individuals usually end up utterly confused and unable to distinguish the difference between love and lust, what's real and what's not.

No longer able to fight against the impulses and strong urges that come with the homosexual lifestyle, they yield, and there begins the seemingly never ending journey of deception, lies, and pain. Following after is, separation from the true inner being as they feel the need to hide their life choice from family, friends and others.

Can they function in society?

YES, they can! Will they be able to operate at maximum potential as complete and whole individuals? One can only speculate.

Let's have a baby

At the crux of the homosexual debate is the scientific fact that every man, woman, boy, and girl was born out of an intimate, monogamous, relationship between a male and a female.

There has never been a known case of humanity where two men or two women fell in love and decided to have a baby by having sexual intercourse.

It is amazing that not one homosexual or lesbian was born out of such a relationship.

James and Jessica

I am reminded of the story of a young man named James, who decided to go through a sex change operation only to fall madly in love with a lesbian named Jessica. They decided to stay together as male and female while assuming the role of the other gender.

That is confusion at a heightened state. A male decides to be female, and a female chooses to be male only to meet one another, fall in love and live together as the other gender. Can we call them homosexual or just confused?

Today same-sex couples can now legally be married and adopt children in many places around the world.

How will those children interpret life? Will they grow up with a healthy understanding of what life and relationships are meant to be?

Children are incredibly impressionable and as a result, learn behaviors by observance and mere everyday exposure. In many cases, it is far too early to tell what the effect will be on these young lives, as this is a relatively new occurrence. The other question is, is it fair to the child?

My dad is now a woman?

Growing up, I had a friend with whom I played little league baseball. One day a car pulled up at the playground, and out of the car came a very muscular man wearing a wig, makeup, dress and high heels.

He proceeded to call out the name of my friend shouting in a baritone voice, "Bobby! it's your mother dear."

Bobby turned red as a tomato. He quickly dropped the bat and ran to the car and left with the man.

Well, at that point all playing of baseball stopped as we were confused and shocked.

Bobby was our friend, and we wanted to know what was going on. At the time I said we were concerned. Now I say we were just plain old nosy.

The next day we got a chance to speak to Bobby and asked him, who was the person that came to pick him up. He took a deep breath and looked at us saying "that was my father." Not many days after, we never saw Bobby again.

I always wondered, was he so embarrassed that he decided to not show up again? Last I heard he went to live with his grandmother.

How was he affected by this change his father had undergone? It must have been devastating growing up with a man you knew as your dad, whom one day started dressing like a woman and calling himself your mother.

There are many children who also had to face such a challenge as their parents male and female decided, it was time for them to embrace their secret feelings and just come out of the closet.

Homosexuality is now being defined in many different ways. The truth of the matter is all of us have been affected by these new revelations of such relationships within our societies.

Can I be a gay Christian?

A modern day phenomenon, is it ok to be gay and Christian?

First let's take a look at the definition of Christianity; it is to live a life free from the entanglements of this world that would cause one to be separated from the Creator, Father God.

Secondly, it is to conform to the teachings of Jesus Christ as noted in the Bible.

It is not just living a life of what's considered right from wrong, but living a life that fulfills God's will on the earth, and to complete the purpose for which you have been born.

Christianity teaches that relationships between persons of the same sex are in fact against the laws of God and are therefore forbidden.

The account of Sodom and Gomorrah in the Bible shows us the displeasure of God and his response in destroying the entire city and all of its inhabitants because they chose to engage in same-sex relationships.

Although the teachings of Christianity forbid such relationships, it provides repentance, forgiveness, healing and deliverance from all such lifestyles. Also note: **true Christianity is not a religion, but rather a way of life.**

No one who chooses Jesus as Lord and Savior is exempt from the Grace and Mercy of God.

There are scores of individuals within the body of Christ who are now living victorious lives after previously living a homosexual lifestyle.

That tells me it can be done. I believe any time we have such a point of reference in any area of life it lends itself to the word of God which states,

"God is no respecter of persons."

If he did it for one, he could do it for all!

Was King James Homosexual?

Why is it that often things we should know, are purposely hidden from us?

Who gains when we ignore issues that we will one day have to confront? The answer is no one!

What would have happened if it were general public knowledge that King James, whose version of the Bible is so prevalent, was indeed bisexual?

History notates that King James preferred the company of a male rather than that of a female.

It is further documented that King James fell in love with his cousin Esme Stuart whom the King made the Duke of Lennox.

There are several other notable and ordinary men confirmed as being lovers of King James. He seemingly was publicly open concerning his relationships.

As a result, he was kidnaped in 1582 while being forced to put forth a proclamation denouncing his lover, which led to Esme Stuart being sent back to France.

The King James Version of the Bible was completed in the year 1611. Although the book bears his name he was not the author or interpreter. He merely commissioned those responsible for putting forth this version.

Approximately 47 biblical scholars, known as the best in their field, submitted to the painstaking work of interpreting the Holy Bible.

The goal was to produce an English version of the entire Bible, which would be entirely parallel to the original Hebrew and Greek writings.

There was to be no compromising of the original Bible. Later this new Bible would be used in all churches replacing what was known as the Bishops Bible.

The men responsible for this new version of the Bible included bishops, linguists and translators from Oxford, Westminster, and Cambridge Universities.

Delivered from, Sent to

I believe some the greatest voices of deliverance in this area will and must come from one who himself has been entangled and now is free.

Who else can carefully maneuver the pathways of this way of life, but someone and those who knew it all too well?

There is yet much fear and misunderstanding in this area; the day will come when we will see multitudes running to places of true healing, restoration, and transformation. Everyone will be able to come with open arms, without fear of being turned away.

Although the face of homosexuality has changed, its impact on the world remains the same. We must be more open than any time before, endeavoring to leave no person behind.

Love You To Death?

Is there such a thing as too much LOVE?

I've never seen or heard of anyone dying from being loved too much. The next time you hear the statement "Love you to death" Stop and think: <u>LOVE</u> only gives or breeds <u>LIFE</u>. God, the Creator, is Love, and He is the source of all Love.

As you look at all of creation, it is plain to see that only a loving creative and concerned creator could have put all of this in motion. He has in fact placed everything we will ever need at our disposal. Also, He has given us the wisdom to travel to other planets and conquer any obstacle man can face.

Within the last 100 years of civilization, we have grown faster than in the last few thousand.

Knowledge increases daily, and new developments and inventions are discovered daily. Maybe this challenge is no different from any other, or is it?

If we can find the cure for cancer and take medication to regulate blood pressure, can we exercise and just see it melt away? Can we wish it away, talk it away or just pray it away?

It takes a combination of many things including prayer to bring someone to the place of true deliverance in this and all areas of life.

Firstly, the person has to have a sincere desire to be free. It cannot be a case of doing it to satisfy the desires of others, but rather, a personal goal. Accountability is also necessary for the changing of daily habits and rituals.

To accomplish a different outcome you must do things differently. Friends and acquaintances may have to change. Places you frequent may also have to change. Imagine the scenario of the former alcoholic thinking he can still go to the bar and hang out with his old friends because he has decided he no longer likes drinking.

This person is marked for failure because he did not recognize the power of influence.

Going back will only awaken the very things he no longer wishes to do. His actions did not line up with his stated desire or words.

**To be successful in anything, what you
do must line up with your words.**

There must be a written plan put forth for you to follow, even the charting of daily progress is necessary.

If you do not have a plan, then your plan is to fail!

Doctor, can I die from this?

In a land of liberty and justice for all, is it possible that this freedom and justice has now become a snare? Faced with the pressures of people wanting more, laws have been passed making what once was deemed as wrong, earthly legal.

In all reality, there are some things a man cannot change or tamper with no matter how hard he tries.

As long as his actions are against the laws of nature, which coincidentally are subject to the legislation of Creator, it will always emphatically be illegal and not prevail.

A matter of life and death!

In the quest to tamper with forbidden fruit, we have come to know AIDS and other STD's.

Some of the symptoms include infections of the windpipe and mouth coupled with labored breathing, high fever, dry cough and white spots on the skin of the genitals and mouth.

There is also a skin tumor called Kaposi's sarcoma and a virus called cytomegalovirus that resembles mononucleosis that often goes unnoticed.

Gay bowel syndrome- Consist of bacteria such as Shigella sonnei, Shigella flexneri, Campylobacter enteritis, Salmonella enteritis, or Campylobacter jejuni. Also noted are intestinal parasites such as Giardia lamblia, Entamoeba histolytica, Entamoeba Coli; Chlamydia trachomatis and Herpes simplex.

These infections can be traced to exposure to fecal material entering the anus or mouth through sexual acts.

In the 1970's health officials in New York City grew concerned about many cases of dysentery within the Greenwich Village community.

Subsequently, an inspection of the water supply was done, and no sign of raw sewage was found. As a result, it was ruled out as the source of the outbreak.

After further investigation and testing, health officials discovered the homosexual behavior of the community was the actual origin and the reason for the epidemic.

Violated

The violated often are those who are weak in mind and or spirit. They never see the violator as they make their approach. It usually starts out being unnoticeable, and always escalates with time.

There are cases in which the violated are forced. However, both situations are traumatic and can be devastating to one's entire psyche.

Often they are left questioning their sexuality; and they end up facing a lifetime or many years of depressed, suicidal thoughts, feeling lonely as though they are left out and forgotten.

These individuals are often afraid of being alone for fear of the tormenting memories. They are frequently in a state of constant denial prone to suicidal tendencies and many emotional challenges.

Recognizing the violated can be a difficult task. Most choose not to reveal their plight while others surround themselves with friends, and some have no friends at all.

What's alarming is that those closest to you are often the last to know or recognize you have been violated. As a parent, you need to ask any and all questions possible in addition to remembering to **keep the lines of communication open!**

A parent's worst nightmare is to find out his child has been violated or molested. I stand firm in believing, prevention is better than cure. You can stop a thing before it ever gets started by being proactive.

You will not see everything

Years ago I was sitting in my office, talking to one of the Ministers of the Church I pastored.

He began telling me about his little ten-year-old daughter Candy.

She was in the backyard playing with one of the neighborhood girls jumping on the trampoline. After about a half hour, he decided to check on the girls, hearing no noise for some time.

As he opened the back door to his amazement, he saw the two girls tightly clenched as they passionately kissed one another. Needless to say, he immediately interrupted the activities and sent the girl home.

He supposedly kept his daughter sheltered from such things, but now she had been exposed or maybe even violated.

My question is, **was it the first time?** There is no telling what kind of effect that little experience can have on an impressionable young mind. That is why, constant reassurance and persistent co-mingling with your children is a must. They must experience healthy holistic relationships to distinguish what one is.

As leaders, parents, caregivers, grandparents and loved ones, we have a great responsibility to teach our children by showing them goodly examples.

Never assume everything is under control and going smoothly, although this may be the case. Always endeavor to stay accessible. Someone may be in need of comfort, instruction, direction or correction.

What will people say?

Don't worry about those who are going to be critical of your stance in this area. Aren't we living in the land of free speech and personal conviction?

These are days in which we must have a genuine concern for mankind as we lay down our differences. Then and only then will we begin to experience great deliverance in our Churches, Communities, and Nations.

After all, is it not true that **we are created to BE? Be authentic, true to self and the Creator.**

We, therefore, must be led by a true Spirit of Love, Peace and justice in all we do. There will always be those who critique and question our methods and motives. The fact remains, we do not answer to them. Our accountability is towards our Creator, one another and those we serve.

**Every wise son is one who endures to the end
of his life's journey, expecting to hear the
voice of the father say "Well done!"**

**Live life to its fullest, mean to make a difference in
all you do by living on and with purpose in mind.**

Even when the music of life stops playing, dance as though it never ceased. There is always someone watching and waiting on the sideline observing every move. They will either be discouraged or encouraged and inspired by what you say and do.

There will also be times of great challenges and crisis, be strong and you will always rise with every storm. Our strength is increased when we trust He who created us. Faith always rises to the occasion, in the midst of confusion and fear.

Your greatest fear should be, not fulfilling the Purpose for which you have been given life!

Be true to self! Don't let it happen to you.

Who then has the answer?

Is there a physiologist, counselor, social worker, probation officer, psychologist, therapist, support program or group with all the answers needed to ensure deliverance from homosexuality?

The answer is no!

Help me, I'm bleeding to death!

There was a woman with an issue of always bleeding in **Matthew 9:20-22**. This woman's suffering grew worse with every visit to the doctor. For 12 long years she sought conventional methods for her **dis-ease,** but only grew worse. No one knew how to stop her bleeding and with every effort, she found herself hemorrhaging to death daily.

I often wondered, did she have a family, and if so what were they going through and how were they dealing with the plight of their loved one.

She ended up spending all she had. With nothing else to give she became desperate to the point of no return.

One day she overheard talk about a man named Jesus, a healer of the sick who was scheduled to come down her street. I am sure she made up in her mind that she was not going to miss this golden opportunity.

As a result, she positioned herself inconspicuously in the crowd. She believed that all she had to do was touch the hem of his garment, and she would be made entirely whole.

She knew all of the time where her deliverance was. After years of suffering and becoming financially depleted, she now only had faith in God to count on rather than her resources.

As Jesus came by, she pressed her way through the crowd eventually touching him.

It is said that instantly she was made whole. There was something about her touch. Jesus recognized, with all of the people touching him, someone had made a withdrawal of healing virtue from him without even asking.

Her faith had made her whole!

Many who are suffering are just like this woman. Trusting everything else until it is all is gone. The tragedy is, many die before ever getting the help they need. Jesus went to them, should we not also follow his perfect example?

I am not saying go into the bars and clubs, but rather be more open and ready to reach out to anyone who may be in need. Jesus made himself available. As a result, all who came to him were healed from all of their Diseases.

He is the shepherd that responds to the cries of his sheep. His Love for us is great, and we

never have to worry about him leaving us for another. That is why you were created distinctly different from any other creature or creation of God.

"There is no one else like you."

If you are reading this book and have struggled with this lifestyle, feeling alienated, dejected and or reject.

Please know that there are individuals and groups that are vastly trying to bridge the gaps and answer the questions and issues that have kept us apart for so long.

I believe there are definite answers to all questions of life that affect us. I hope we continue to strive towards understanding and oneness, as we tear down lines of discrimination and hatred seeking real resolve in the Spirit of LOVE.

The intent of this book was to ask many piercing questions while looking forensically at the topic of Homosexuality.

However, the title stemmed from many years of research and just asking the same questions over and over again to people from all walks of life from all over the world.

One day as I was addressing a small group of individuals I noticed a young man listening rather attentively.

At the end of the session, this same person blurted out, "So it's not what you think it is!"

That was my Eureka moment. I then realized that people were confused and didn't quite understand the meaning of homosexuality.

I've had the passion for bringing clarity concerning this issue to the Church as well as the general public for over 15 years.

My hope is to bring better understand of how to deal with this matter in every situation.

I trust this book has educated and provoked a healthy interest in the subject of Homosexuality. In addition to equipping you with the necessary tools for dealing with people who may be different from yourself in our societies.

It is time for healing and reconciliation as we all come together united in the true Spirit of "Philadelphia" Brotherhood and Brotherly Love.

"HOMOSEXUALITY"
IS IT WHAT YOU
THINK IT IS?

Cited Works

*Page-6: The First Public Debate about Homosexuality in England: The Case of Captain Jones, 1772
CITATION: Rictor Norton (Ed.), *Homosexuality in Eighteenth-Century England: A Sourcebook.* Updated 15 April 2015 <http://rictornorton.co.uk/eighteen/>.

*Page 9: Judit Takács: The Double Life of Kertbeny In: G. Hekma (ed.) Past and Present of Radical Sexual Politics, UvA – Mosse Foundation, Amsterdam, 2004. Kertbeny and homosexuality

*Page 14: Intercrural sex /From Wikipedia, the free encyclopedia

+ Chisholm, Hugh, ed. (1911). "Niam-Niam". *Encyclopedia Britannica* (11th ed.). Cambridge University Press.
+ Evans-Pritchard, E. E. (1979) "Witchcraft Explains Unfortunate Events" in William A. Lessa and Evon Z. Vogt (eds.) *Reader in Comparative Religion. An anthropological approach. Fourth Edition.* New York: Harper Collins Publishers. pp. 362–366
+ Evans-Pritchard, E. E. (1967) *the Zande Trickster.* Oxford: Clarendon Press.
+ Evans-Pritchard, E. E.1937 *Witchcraft, Oracles and Magic among the Azande.* Oxford University Press. 1976 abridged edition: ISBN 0-19-874029-8

*Page 123: ↕ Bergeron, David M. King James and Letters of Homoerotic Desire, Iowa City: University of Iowa P, 1999

> Template: UK-noble-stub Template: Start box Template: Succession box Template: End box Template: Earls of Lennoxde: Esmé Stewart, 1. Duke of Lennox es: Esmé Estuardo

*KJV: Bible

*Dale O'Leary

*The material presented here was collected by members of the National Association of Research and Therapy of Homosexuality, NARTH

*Article by: Fathers for Life — Fathers' and Men's issues are everyone's issues

*Shilts, R. (1987) *and the Band Played On.* NY: St. Martins Press.

*Markell, E., Haven, R., Kuritsubo, R. (1983) Intestinal Parasitic Infection In Homosexual Men at a San Francisco Health Fair. *Western Journal of Medicine.* 139: 177 - 178.

About the Author

Dr. R Phillip Mitchell is a visionary, builder, humanitarian, author, and artist and a man who simply loves people. As a bishop and senior pastor, he has traveled abroad, establishing schools, communities, businesses, and churches nationally and internationally. He is the founding visionary of New Beginning Ministries Intl. and All Nations Intl. Fellowship.

His heart is in seeing the fulfillment of the divine purpose in the lives of the people he serves. In addition, over the last fifteen years, he has hosted his own radio broadcasts, entitled Sound the Alarm Broadcast and Prophetic Insight, as well as a television broadcast, entitled Teen Talk.

Happily married for twenty-plus years, Dr. Mitchell is a proud father, grandfather, and great-grandfather.

Lastly, Dr. Mitchell is a former member of the United States Armed Services, having honorably served and retired as a US Marine.

Notes

Notes

Printed in the United States
By Bookmasters